Instant Magento Performance Optimization How-to

Improve the performance of your Magento stores using practical, hands-on recipes

Nayrolles Mathieu

[PACKT] PUBLISHING

BIRMINGHAM - MUMBAI

Instant Magento Performance Optimization How-to

First published: February 2013

Production Reference: 1150213

Published by Packt Publishing Ltd.
Livery Place
35 Livery Street
Birmingham B3 2PB, UK.

ISBN 978-1-78216-542-2

www.packtpub.com

Credits

Author
Nayrolles Mathieu

Reviewer
Milan Kumar Saha

Acquisition Editor
James Keane

Commissioning Editor
Yogesh Dalvi

Technical Editors
Hardik Soni

Pooja Prakashan

Copy Editor
Aditya Nair

Project Coordinator
Sneha Modi

Proofreader
Kelly Hutchinson

Graphics
Valentina D'silva

Production Coordinators
Conidon Miranda

Nilesh R. Mohite

Cover Work
Conidon Miranda

Cover Image
Conidon Miranda

About the Author

Nayrolles Mathieu was born in France, and it is where he started his studies in Computing Sciences at eXia.Cesi and passed the Diploma in Information Systems Management. He travelled to Europe and completed various internships, where he learned how to optimize in industrial environments.

In the fourth year, he decided to pursue a double diploma course at UQAM, Québec, Canada. During his study at UQAM, he was awarded for one of his publications, *Specification and Detection of SOA Antipatterns*, in the 10th International Conference on Service-Oriented Computing. He is still completing his last year in both schools, and has written two Master's theses in the Artificial Intelligence and Quality fields.

He has worked for companies worldwide, such as Eurocopter and Saint-Gobain. Currently, he is giving courses on agile development, service-oriented architectures, business intelligence, and data mining at the bachelor level in UQAM and eXia.Cesi, along with his own studies.

You can find out more about him on his website, www.mathieu-nayrolles.com.

I would like to thank Packt Publishing's team for their support, and in particular Veena Manjrekar for giving me the opportunity to write this book, Yogesh Dalvi for helping me define the content's headings, and Sneha Modi for bringing this book to you.

I would like to thank Lakmé Gremillet and Brian Vowles from CYRRHUS – innovative training paths, for their support and their precious reviews on this book. Without them, this book would definitely have never seen the light of day.

About the Reviewer

Milan Kumar Saha is a software engineer living in Bangladesh. Over the last 5 years, he has worked with many distributed systems based on open source technologies such as PHP, CakePHP, Zend, and CodeIgnitor. He has hands-on experience in developing successful e-commerce solutions using Magento and Zen Cart. He is a Git lover whose recent passions includes Python and mobile application development using the Android SDK.

www.PacktPub.com

Support files, eBooks, discount offers and more

You might want to visit www.PacktPub.com for support files and downloads related to your book.

Did you know that Packt offers eBook versions of every book published, with PDF and ePub files available? You can upgrade to the eBook version at www.PacktPub.com and as a print book customer, you are entitled to a discount on the eBook copy. Get in touch with us at service@packtpub.com for more details.

At www.PacktPub.com, you can also read a collection of free technical articles, sign up for a range of free newsletters and receive exclusive discounts and offers on Packt books and eBooks.

http://PacktLib.PacktPub.com

Do you need instant solutions to your IT questions? PacktLib is Packt's online digital book library. Here, you can access, read and search across Packt's entire library of books.

Why Subscribe?

- ▶ Fully searchable across every book published by Packt
- ▶ Copy and paste, print and bookmark content
- ▶ On demand and accessible via web browser

Free Access for Packt account holders

If you have an account with Packt at www.PacktPub.com, you can use this to access PacktLib today and view nine entirely free books. Simply use your login credentials for immediate access.

Table of Contents

Preface

In the open source, e-commerce platforms community, users and developers have only one word to say: Magento! Indeed, in a short period of time, Magento has established itself as the most popular e-commerce platform in the market. Moreover, many developers create Magento extensions that can fit most usual and unusual needs.

Magento Inc. claims that they are trusted by more than 125,000 businesses, including some major brands such as Nike and Lenovo and was downloaded over 3.8 million times. From the beginning, there are two versions of the Magento platform, the Community and the Enterprise version. The Enterprise version has annual fees starting from USD 14,000 (December 2012), while the Community edition remains free. It is likely that the Community version is the most used of both.

One hundred twenty-five thousand merchants all around the world and 3.8 million downloads are quite impressive statistics, but how to explain the gap between people who try to create their own businesses and people who actually have a profitable e-commerce out there? Magento is an advanced e-commerce platform, and advanced also means a complex platform. Like any complex platform for online businesses, Magento configurations must evolve to fit new user requirements and operational needs. The changes resulting from the increasing number of browsers and buyers may degrade the quality of service and the user experience of any e-commerce website. The optimization of an attractive commercial website is a nontrivial task that deserves time and knowledge. Moreover, the optimization is a critical point for all growing businesses, because a misconfiguration could make you lose money, a lot of money. Indeed, if your server is overloaded, even for a short period of time, a browser that wants to turn into a buyer will not be able to do it; and it's good to know that, on an average, a dissatisfied customer will talk to twelve people about his bad experience while a satisfied customer will only talk to three.

There are numerous other causes that lead to giving up Magento or making you lose money, such as getting lost inside the tons of files, being disturbed by the massive object programming style, or becoming tired of trying configurations found online that do not work. However, we will focus on performance optimization.

Despite all these traps, the good news is that there are hundreds of people like you and I, who have made their own mistakes, created best practices, and shared all this knowledge on the Internet.

Instant Magento Performance Optimization How-to has been designed to be a reference for administrators and developers on how to turn your businesses into performances, by reducing a huge amount of time in online research and unsuccessful attempts.

Although the optimization is a nontrivial and complex task, I want this book to be easily accessible for anyone who wants to speed up his Magento; that's why I have spent dozens and dozens of hours in researching, testing, and building simple step-by-step tutorials.

This book will focus on the latest release of the Magento Community Edition, Version 1.7. Various tricks and tips exposed in this book will certainly work with earlier versions, especially Version 1.6, but I can't guarantee it for all of them. Moreover, if your Magento Community version isn't the latest one, we recommend as a first step to upgrade it for optimization, security, and innovation reasons.

What this book covers

Merging CSS files (Must know) shows you how to gather all the CSS files scattered over your Magento, which will optimize the loading time in a way you wouldn't expect.

Merging JavaScript (Must know) shows you how to merge JavaScript files inside a unique file, in the same way as CSS files.

Logging files (Must know) explains that for every main action your Magento has done, it has to write a line on your hard drive in order to help you monitor your e-commerce. Nevertheless, this feature is really resource-consuming.

Compiling (Must know) introduces you to the lookup, which is a process that finds PHP files (that Magento are mainly composed of) in your web server. We can help this process to run faster using compilation.

Managing the index (Must know) introduces you to the index, which is a data structure that accelerates the retrieving process of the information present in your database.

Removing PayPal's logo (Must know) explains how easy it is to make money through PayPal. Unfortunately, retrieving the logo from their website takes a while. That's why we will remove it and display a locally-hosted image instead.

Using the Magento caching system (Must know) introduces you to Magento's built-in caching system for saving frequently asked requests.

Enhancing the expiration date (Should know) shows you that browsers can save some of your website content, such as images and scripts. This recipe explains how to encourage them to save it for a longer time.

Keeping your connections alive (Should know) shows you how customers accede to your e-commerce through HTTP and TCP connections. We will manage to proceed many HTTP connections in one TCP connection.

Storing your sessions in the database (Should know) shows you that when a client comes back to your website after a few days, he will still have information such as shopping carts intact.

Configuring MySQL (Should know) explains how MySQL is provided with settings in order to make it work on every computer. Improve the settings for your hardware.

Using a memory-based filesystem for caching (Become an expert) introduces you to the slowest component of a computer, the hard drive, and how Magento makes massive use of it. This lets you use your available RAM.

Compressing your code – gzip (Become an expert) walks you through the compression algorithms created for plain text that can be used to compress all your codes files.

Installing a PHP accelerator (Become an expert) explains that PHP is a language that can be transformed, on demand, to be understandable by your processors. We can save this transformation.

Clustering (Become an expert) shows you how to configure a set of loosely connected computers working together for handling more and more customers.

Balancing load (Become an expert) explains how to dynamically redirect your customers towards the least loaded servers.

Replicating the database (Become an expert) shows you how to create multiple nodes for storing systems so as to optimize the reading and writing of data.

Checking the configuration (Must know) explains how to identify common misconfigurations.

Clearing caches (Must know) explains how to clear all your caches in order to start afresh.

Logging (Must know) shows you how to find all your log files in your filesystem.

Using template hints (Must know) explains how to display template-related information for debugging purposes.

Using the Profiler (Should know) explains how to use the Profiler. Profiler is a monitoring system used to measure time on your Magento.

Using a debugger (Should know) explains how to analyze your code step-by-step if all the information you have does not tell you where the bugs are.

What you need for this book

The most important prerequisite you must have before reading this book is the kind of courage that enables you to get away with murder when you are inside a management system.

A test subject for testing and optimization is of course required, and it will be a plus if the reader is accustomed to the technical backend console; but it's not necessary.

In order to follow the optimizations present in this book, you will need a copy of your actual website or a fresh installation of the Magento Community Edition with the sample data. Of course, you can apply these optimizations on your live websites, but at your own risk. Indeed, beginning such optimizations can (always) create some mess.

Who this book is for

This book is specially made for Magento administrators and users who are familiar with using the backend technical console, but people who are new to anything beyond this and wish to optimize their online store for increasing performance can also read this book.

Anyway, if you are interested in building a robust e-commerce business and intend to really satisfy customers beyond the average, you definitely need to read this book.

Conventions

In this book, you will find a number of styles of text that distinguish between different kinds of information. Here are some examples of these styles, and an explanation of their meaning.

Code words in text are shown as follows: "The Magento Core adds an HTML `<div>` tag before each file."

A block of code is set as follows:

```
<connection>|
    <host>|<![CDATA[NEW_SERVER_ADDRESS]]>|</host>|
    <username>|<![CDATA[NEW_USER_NAME]]>|</username>|
    <password>|<![CDATA[NEW_PASSWORD]]>|</password>|
    <dbname>|<![CDATA[NEW DATABASE_NAME]]>|</dbname>|
    <initStatements>|<![CDATA[SET NAMES utf8]]>|</initStatements>|
    <model>|<![CDATA[mysql4]]>|</model>|
    <type>|<![CDATA[pdo_mysql]]>|</type>|
    <pdoType>|<![CDATA[]]>|</pdoType>|
    <active>|1</active>|
</connection>|
```

When we wish to draw your attention to a particular part of a code block, the relevant lines or items are set in bold:

```
<default_read>
<connection>
    <host><![CDATA[SLAVE_SERVER_ADDRESS]]></host>
    <username><![CDATA[SLAVE_USER_NAME]]></username>
    <password><![CDATA[SLAVE_PASSWORD]]></password>
    <dbname><![CDATA[SLAVE_DATABASE_NAME]]></dbname>
    <initStatements><![CDATA[SET NAMES utf8]]></initStatements>
    <model><![CDATA[mysql4]]></model>
    <type><![CDATA[pdo_mysql]]></type>
    <pdoType><![CDATA[]]></pdoType>
    <active>1</active>
</connection>
</default_read>
```

Any command-line input or output is written as follows:

```
sudo pecl install xdebug
```

New terms and **important words** are shown in bold. Words that you see on the screen, in menus or dialog boxes for example, appear in the text like this: "Finally click on the **Submit** button."

> Tips and tricks appear like this.

Reader feedback

Feedback from our readers is always welcome. Let us know what you think about this book—what you liked or may have disliked. Reader feedback is important for us to develop titles that you really get the most out of.

To send us general feedback, simply send an e-mail to `feedback@packtpub.com`, and mention the book title via the subject of your message.

If there is a book that you need and would like to see us publish, please send us a note in the **SUGGEST A TITLE** form on `www.packtpub.com` or e-mail `suggest@packtpub.com`.

If there is a topic that you have expertise in and you are interested in either writing or contributing to a book, see our author guide on `www.packtpub.com/authors`.

Customer support

Now that you are the proud owner of a Packt book, we have a number of things to help you to get the most from your purchase.

Errata

Although we have taken every care to ensure the accuracy of our content, mistakes do happen. If you find a mistake in one of our books—maybe a mistake in the text or the code—we would be grateful if you would report this to us. By doing so, you can save other readers from frustration and help us improve subsequent versions of this book. If you find any errata, please report them by visiting http://www.packtpub.com/support, selecting your book, clicking on the **errata submission form** link, and entering the details of your errata. Once your errata are verified, your submission will be accepted and the errata will be uploaded on our website, or added to any list of existing errata, under the Errata section of that title. Any existing errata can be viewed by selecting your title from http://www.packtpub.com/support.

Piracy

Piracy of copyright material on the Internet is an ongoing problem across all media. At Packt, we take the protection of our copyright and licenses very seriously. If you come across any illegal copies of our works, in any form, on the Internet, please provide us with the location address or website name immediately so that we can pursue a remedy.

Please contact us at copyright@packtpub.com with a link to the suspected pirated material.

We appreciate your help in protecting our authors, and our ability to bring you valuable content.

Questions

You can contact us at questions@packtpub.com if you are having a problem with any aspect of the book, and we will do our best to address it.

Instant Magento Performance Optimization How-to

Welcome to *Instant Magento Performance Optimization How-to*. This book will teach you how to turn your online business into a high performance money-making machine by saving you a huge amount of time in online research and unsuccessful attempts.

This book covers all the most popular best practices that can be applied for speeding up your Magento. All tricks and tips shown in this book come with the Magento backend, therefore you don't need to be a Magento expert, or even a master user, to apply them on your website.

All the experiments shown in this book have been released with the latest Magento Community Edition (Version 1.7.0.2, at the time of writing) setup and the Sample Data provided by Magento Inc. (Version 1.6.1.0). The displayed results are provided by different tools, but the main ones are Pingdom tools, Mozilla Firebug, Google Speed Tracer, and Google PageSpeed.

The results are shown in terms of seconds and milliseconds (1 second = 1000 milliseconds), kiloctet (1 megaoctet = 1000 kiloctet and 1000 megaoctet = 1 gigaoctet), and the number of requests. The number of requests represent the amount of files your future customer's browser has to retrieve from your Magento website.

We recommend that you follow our experiments step-by-step. In which case, you should prepare a copy of your current Magento store or set up the same test subject that we did.

First, we would like to introduce you to the measures of performance that will be used throughout the book. The results that you can see in the following table are the ones before any tweaking is done. These come from our test subject, which refers to a classic installation.

Type	Requests	Load time	Size
Overall	49	2.58 seconds	724.3 KB
CSS	3	107 milliseconds	100.6 KB
JS	13	742 milliseconds	363.4 KB

As you can see, our website is fully loaded in 2.58 seconds and 49 requests. This length of time is unacceptable when there is a unique user on our website.

Can you imagine the loading time if 10 or 100 users are trying to access your website at the same time? Forty-nine requests also seem disproportionate for only loading the home page.

In this section, we will play with five common settings to accelerate your business, CSS and JavaScript merging, log, compilation, and indexing. For each new task, we will turn off the previous settings in order to clearly identify what the bonuses are for each one.

Before tweaking your Magento, you should do a little work. These are not Magento specifics but general web optimization practices:

- ▶ **Get a dedicated server**: Most of the hosting enterprises will gather your website with hundreds of others. If you are on a mutual hosting platform, your performance will depend on other websites' traffic.

- ▶ **Hosting country**: Choose a hosting company that owns servers in the country where your customers are, and not necessarily the best ones in the market.

- ▶ **Versions**: Always update your servers with the latest versions, with updated versions come features, security, and performance.

- ▶ **Images**: Always rasterize your images to the size you want them to be displayed and crop all white spaces. Go for PNG or GIF files instead of JPG files.

- ▶ **Extensions and modules**: Disable any extensions or modules that you don't use.

Merging CSS files (Must know)

In this recipe we will learn how to merge all CSS files that are present in your Magento.

How to do it...

First, we will merge all CSS files together. In order to do it, go to your backend and then navigate to **System | Configuration | Advanced | Developer| CSS Settings**.

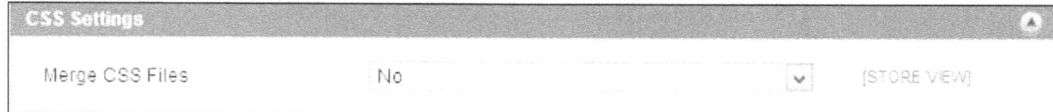

CSS Settings			
Merge CSS Files	No	⌄	[STORE VIEW]

You just have to turn on the **Merge CSS Files** setting and save your settings in the top-right corner. The following table shows you the difference after the previous change, that is, after CSS merging. For every single change in your Magento configuration, we will provide a similar table.

Type	Requests	Load time	Size
CSS (before)	3	107 milliseconds	100.6 KB
CSS (after)	1	73 milliseconds	110.6 KB

As you can see, it's not marvellous but it is the beginning of optimization, and any load time or requests you obtain are beneficial.

How it works...

The functioning principle of this basic option is very simple. Basically, the Magento core is able to find and merge together all CSS files discovered in your website. This technique reduces the number of requests by the previous number of CSS files.

There's more...

In this section, we will show you how to go beyond the simple check-and-save settings shown previously. Indeed, you can format your CSS files manually to obtain better performance.

CSS compression

When you write your cascading stylesheet, you certainly put the following syntax into a priority list:

```
/* Headings */
h1,h2,h3,
h4,h5,h6      { margin:0 0 5px; line-height:1.35; }
h1            { font-size:20px; font-weight:normal; }
h2            { font-size:18px; font-weight:normal; }
h3            { font-size:16px; font-weight:bold; }
h4            { font-size:14px; font-weight:bold; }
h5            { font-size:12px; font-weight:bold; }
h6            { font-size:11px; font-weight:bold; }
```

Believe it or not, this bunch of code can be optimized a lot. Of course, the optimization comes with a total destruction of readability, as shown in the following code snippet:

```
h1{font-size:20px;font-weight:400}h1,h2,h3,h4,h5,h6{color:#0a263c;
line-height:1.35;margin:0 0 5px}h2{font-size:18px;font-weight:400}
h3{font-size:16px;font-weight:700}h4{font-size:14px;font-weight:700}
h5{font-size:12px;font-weight:700}h6{font-size:11px;font-weight:700}
```

Using this way of coding, we have optimized our CSS file by 36.22 percent (67 characters less). To do it you have to sort selectors and properties and compress colors and font weight. When it's done, you have to remove all backslashes, spaces, and new lines.

The good news is that you don't need to do it by hand. There's an excellent website that can do it for you: `http://compressmycode.com`.

Merging JavaScript (Must know)

In the same way as CSS, we can merge all JavaScript files in our Magento.

How to do it...

In order to merge your JavaScript files, you have to open your Magento backend and go to **System | Configuration | Advanced | Developer | JavaScript Settings**.

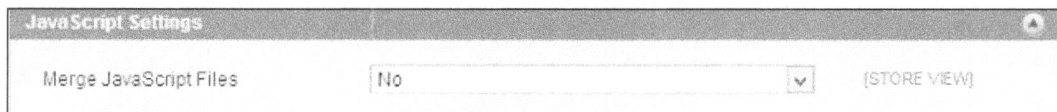

JavaScript Settings			
Merge JavaScript Files	No	⌄	[STORE VIEW]

Just as for the CSS settings, you have to turn this option on and save your settings in the top-right corner. The following table shows you the difference after the JavaScript merging is done.

Type	Requests	Load time	Size
JS (before)	13	742 milliseconds	363.4 KB
JS (after)	1	148 milliseconds	359.9 KB

The overall size is somewhat similar, but the number of requests is now only one and the load time has been reduced by more than half a second. Remember, the overall load time was 2.58 seconds, so this improvement is really significant.

How it works...

The Magento core is able to find and merge all the JavaScript files present in your installation. By reducing the number of files to retrieve you considerably lower the load time, even if the overall size is quite the same.

There's more...

Once again, you can definitely improve your performance by doing a little by hand. In this section, you will learn how to compress your JavaScript files.

Simple JavaScript compression

Analogous to a cascading stylesheet, JavaScript can be compressed by removing spaces, backslashes, and new lines.

```
function displayDate()
{
  document.getElementById("demo").innerHTML=Date();
}
displayDate(){document.getElemById("demo").innerHTML=Date()}
```

The file has been reduced by 5 characters which means 6.49 percent saved. On a very large JavaScript file, such as libraries, this will be very effective.

Base 62 JavaScript compression

The base 62 is a positional notation. A positional notation is a method of representing encoded numbers and it can be used to represent a very long test by a shorter version. Using the base 62 will reduce the time to download the file but will add an extra step before the customer can use it. Indeed, the client has to decode the encoded JavaScript. The previous function in base 62 is equal to the following function:

```
eval(function(p,a,c,k,e,r){e=String;if[…]))
```

For the sake of readability, we will not put the whole of base 62 encoding here. But, before applying this technique to your JavaScript files, you have to compare the reduction in time for downloading the script to the extra time taken to execute it.

Including other libraries

There are some known issues when you use JavaScript merging and other JavaScript libraries ,such as jQuery integrated in Magento. Most of the time the issues come from bad integration.

Logging files (Must know)

For every move of your customer, Magento will write a line in specific files. It's not rocket science to assume that this logging process slows it down.

How to do it...

To turn off your logging system, you have to open your Magento backend and go to **System | Configuration | Advanced | Developer | Log Settings**.

Log Settings		
Enabled	No	[STORE VIEW]

Turn off the option and save your settings. The following table shows the data with the log turned off:

Type	Requests	Load time	Size
Overall (before)	49	2.58 seconds	724.3 KB
Overall (after)	49	2.50 seconds	724.3 KB

The difference is negligible on a non-stressed server, but we have to assume that with the increase in the load on the server, this option will be more effective.

How it works...

The log files are located in `{{base_dir}}/var/log` and are divided into two pieces. The first one is the system log file and the second one is the exception log file. Although this file can be useful for debugging and monitoring your Magento website, the operation to write it in the hard drive slows down other operations such as retrieving information for clients.

Compiling (Must know)

The term *compilation* could mislead you if you are used to programming in C or any other compiled language. The Magento compilation we will learn here only gathers PHP files together.

How to do it...

To enable the compilation, navigate to **System | Tool | Compilation**.

Compilation		Run Compilation Process
Compilation State		
Compiler Status	Disabled	
Compilation State	Not Compiled	
Collected Files Count	0	
Compiled Scopes Count	0	
Scopes Compilation Settings	default	

When the page is loaded, click on the **Run Compilation Process** button and wait for a while for the task to be completed. The following table shows the data with compilation enabled:

Type	Requests	Load time	Size
Overall (before)	49	2.58 seconds	724.3 KB
Overall (after)	49	2.18 seconds	724.3 KB

Here we go, another half a second less in comparison with the base test.

How it works...

This option will gather all PHP classes scattered all over the Magento framework into one folder. The main goal is to speed up the look-up process on the server; it is an operation done by the PHP core in order to find dependent classes and libraries scattered all over your server's filesystem. If the files are all together, the look-up operation will be easier.

Managing the index (Must know)

The index is a data structure that helps to retrieve data faster.

How to do it...

To manage Magento indexes, go to **System | Index Management**.

Hit the link, click on **Select All**, and then on the **Submit** button. After a moment, each status turns to green and a message will pop up on the top of the table. This message will be of the form "A total of (x) index(es) have reindexed data".

The following table shows the data with compilation enabled:

Type	Requests	Load time	Size
Overall (before)	49	2.58 seconds	724.3 KB
Overall (after)	49	2.20 seconds	724.3 KB

As you can see in the preceding table, this option reduces the load time by another 0.38 seconds.

How it works...

Magento indexes most of your data in order to access it faster. An index is a data structure that improves the speed for retrieving the data and slows down the writing operation. In the case of an e-commerce website, most of the data operations are that of retrieving (for example, to display products). When you create new articles or categories, you should go back to the **Index Management** page and re-index all your data.

Removing PayPal's logo (Must know)

The display of images from other websites can slow down your whole web page. Indeed, we have to resolve the distant address and then start a new download process from this distant server.

How to do it...

We definitely appreciate how easily we can make money with Magento through PayPal, but let's have a look at PayPal's logo on our website. PayPal's logo is a 160 x 60 GIF image and its size is only 5.3 KB. Nevertheless, this tiny image comes from the PayPal website and it's amazingly slow to get it displayed on our website.

In order to remove it, go to **System | Configuration | Payment Methods | PayPal All-in-One Payment Solutions** and then hit the **Configure** button. In this page, go to **Basic Settings - PayPal Payments Advanced | Advanced Settings | Frontend Experience Settings** and select **No Logo**.

Frontend Experience Settings		
PayPal Product Logo	No Logo ∨ • Displays on catalog pages and homepage.	[STORE VIEW]

Save your configuration in the top-right corner. The following table shows the data for the PayPal logo:

Type	Requests	Load time	Size
With the PayPal logo	37	1.72 seconds	719 KB
Without the PayPal logo	35	1.12 seconds	713.4 KB

More than half a second less on the loading of the home page with this simple setting. Of course, we encourage you to display PayPal's logo on your website; just host it locally.

How it works...

The PayPal logo is hosted on the PayPal website. According to the Pingdom Tools website (http://tools.pingdom.com), the statistics of this image are as follows:

▶ Source: http://www.paypalobjects.com
▶ Weight: 5.3 KB
▶ Size: 150 x 160 pixels
▶ Type: GIF
▶ Total time to retrieve: 1.70 seconds

We will not be able to achieve any less than 1.70 seconds on the loading of the home page because all images are loaded in parallel. The reason this image takes so long to be retrieved from PayPal's servers is because our server has to resolve the real address of the image, and SSL is activated for all communications with PayPal, even for images.

There's more...

Downloading images from the distant server can improve your performance if the distant server is specifically designed to achieve this task.

Using a content delivery network (CDN)

A content delivery network, also known as CDN, is a group of servers scattered all over the world inside data centers in order to deliver static content such as images and style files, in an optimized way. Indeed, your users can have a server belonging to the CDN that is closer than your Magento server, and the CDN servers are optimized for delivering static contents.

Let's have a look at our website if we turn on all the options we have previously studied:

- ▶ Set **Merge CSS Files** to **Yes**
- ▶ Set **Merge JavaScript Files** to **Yes**
- ▶ Set **Log Settings Enabled** to **No**
- ▶ Set **Compilation Enabled** to **Yes**
- ▶ Set **Index up to date** to **Yes**
- ▶ Set **PayPal Logo** to **No**

The following table shows you how much we have improved Magento's performances so far:

Type	Requests	Load time	Size
CSS (before)	3	107 milliseconds	100.6 KB
CSS (after)	1	35 milliseconds	110.6 KB
JS (before)	13	742 milliseconds	363.4 KB
JS (after)	1	62 milliseconds	360 KB
Overall (before)	49	2.58 seconds	724.3 KB
Overall (after)	35	1.12 seconds	713.4 KB

With these six very simple settings, we improve our performance by more than one second.

Nevertheless, 1.12 seconds is still high for an e-commerce website. With the following settings, we will go deeper in order to break the 1-second wall. To do that huge task, we will compress the size of our pages by 80 percent, set up and administrate caching systems, and optimize the way PHP, Apache, and MySQL work.

With the previous settings, we have improved the performance of our test subject by almost 1 second with six simple settings. It's time to go under the surface of Magento and the different servers that support it. As previously done, for each new task we will turn off or reverse the previous settings in order to clearly identify what the pros of each one are. However, all settings seen before are still enabled.

As a reminder, the following table shows our test subjects' performances:

Type	Requests	Load time	Size
CSS	1	35 milliseconds	110.6 KB
JS	1	62 milliseconds	360 KB
Overall	35	1.12 seconds	713.4 KB

We will show you how to parameterize your servers in order to get some speed. We advise you to rename the `local.xml.sample` file inside the `/errors/` directory of Magento to `local.xml`. With this action, you will be able to see errors on your Magento frontend.

We assume that most of the readers are on a Linux-based system. The following is the configuration for this book:

- 2x Ubuntu Server 12.04.1 (32 bit), 2 GB RAM, and 1 Core at 2.7 GHz
- MySQL 14.14
- Apache 2.2.22
- PHP 5.3.10-1

Using the Magento caching system (Must know)

A cache is a system that stores data so that future requests for that data can be served faster. Having cache is definitely a good thing, but the caching system of Magento is not super effective.

How to do it...

Let's begin with cache enabling, even if most users are well aware of th.s ... Go to your backend console and then go to **System | Cache Management**.

By default, all caches are enabled; but some have a negative impact. You have to disable caches for the following items:

- **Collections Data**
- **EAV types and attributes**
- **Web Services Configuration**

The following table shows the improvement made due to the previous settings, that is, by disabling the selected caches:

Type	Requests	Load time	Size
All caches enabled	35	1.12 seconds	713.4 KB
Selected cache enabled	1	903 milliseconds	713.4 KB

Another little win, 200 milliseconds, just enough to fulfill the promise made in the previous recipes.

How it works...

A cache is a system that stores data so that future requests for that data can be served faster. A web cache stores copies of documents passing through it, and subsequent requests may be satisfied from the cache if a set of conditions exists.

There are many hypotheses out there to explain this weird optimization. The main one is that the Magento core has to parse the cache and check in MySQL to compare updated data, and this causes a huge delay. In fact, by allowing Magento to do these kinds of operations, we don't use the full resources of our systems.

Enhancing the expiration date (Should know)

In this recipe, we will use the Apache module Expires in order to maximize the cache utilization.

How to do it...

Open the file named `.htaccess` in the home directory of Magento and go to line 181. Modify lines 181 through 189 so that it looks like the following:

```
<IfModule mod_expires.c>

#############################################
## Add default Expires header
## http://developer.yahoo.com/performance/rules.html#expires
    ExpiresActive On
    ExpiresDefault "access plus 1 month"
</IfModule>
```

How it works...

The Apache Expires module controls the HTTP header named `Expires`. These headers are used to inform the client about the document's validity and persistence. If the requested document is present in one of our cache systems, it will be provided from the cache rather than the filesystem. After a fixed amount of time, one month in this case, the copy is considered expired and a new copy has to be copied into the cache from the original source.

Keeping your connections alive (Should know)

In this recipe, we will use the Apache module KeepAlive to speed up the display process of a web page containing a lot of images.

How to do it...

On a shared hosting environment, it's highly probable that your host has already done this. To check this, use the **Network** tab of Google Chrome Developer tools and look at the **Response** header; you should find a line like the following:

```
Keep-Alive: timeout=15, max=200
```

If this line does not appear, locate the `apache2.conf` file (for us it was under `/etc/apache2/`) on your web server and modify the following lines so it looks like the following:

```
KeepAlive On
KeepAliveTimeout 15
MaxKeepAliveRequests 200
```

This setting can improve the load time by 50 percent for HTML files with a lot of images.

Using the web stressor Apache Bench, we will make 300 requests for a category page (we use the sample data provided by Magento), and display 30 of them per page. That means 30 images to display, plus the basic theme images.

The URL to do the test is `http://YOUR-STORE/index.php/electronics.html?limit=30`.

In order to run this, benchmark yourself. You can run the following command on Linux:

```
sudo ab -n 300 -c 5 http://YOUR-STORE/index.php/electronics.html?limit=30
```

That means 300 requests with five concurrent users.

Type	Min (milliseconds)	Max (milliseconds)	Median (milliseconds)	Request/second
KeepAlive off	444	862	478	1.98
KeepAlive on	432	744	452	2.17

As you can see, the improvements aren't much but we have to assume that we can't see the full power of this setting by stressing our server ourselves. Nevertheless, according to the Page Speed, YSlow, and other tools that aim to optimize websites, this feature is a must-have. Of course, results can change widely considering your hardware.

How it works...

The idea behind the KeepAlive mechanism is to use a single TCP connection for a set of multiple HTTP requests and responses. The aim of this technique is to economize the opening and closing time required for a TCP connection. Indeed, your server will open only one connection and send responses for many requests through it.

Storing your sessions in the database (Should know)

Sessions are mechanisms that allow users to keep their shopping carts safe even if they don't browse our website for a few days. By default, the sessions are saved in the filesystem, and the performance could be improved by storing it in your database.

How to do it...

Open the file named `local.xml` under `app/etc/` and modify line 55 so that it looks like the following line:

```
<session_save><![CDATA[db]]></session_save>
```

How it works...

By default, the sessions are stored in the filesystem under small files, one per session. This option will simply store the contents of these files into the database. This can improve your performance because the database-retrieving process is faster than the filesystem-retrieving process. Another scenario to choose this way of storage is when you have more than one frontend server.

Configuring MySQL (Should know)

The MySQL default configuration is really safe. Indeed, MySQL developers want their product to be run on all servers, even smaller ones. If you have a server with RAM greater than 1 GB, you can definitely improve your MySQL. You can also, periodically, select all the tables in your MySQL Manager and apply the `repair` and `optimize` commands.

How to do it...

Open the file named `my.cnf` in the root directory of your MySQL installation and modify it as follows:

```
key_buffer = 512M
max_allowed_packet = 64M
table_cache = 512
sort_buffer_size = 4M
net_buffer_length = 8K
read_buffer_size = 4M
read_rnd_buffer_size = 2M
myisam_sort_buffer_size = 64M
```

```
tmp_table_size = 128m
query_cache_size = 96m
query_cache_type = 1
thread_cache_size = 8
max_connections = 400
wait_timeout = 300
thread_concurrency = (Computer CPU'S * 2)
```

How it works...

The efficiency of these settings depends on the number of articles and categories present on your website, but the key point is to allow MySQL to use the server's RAM in a more intensive way. When a query is cached, its result (that is, the data sent to the client) is already known and stored somewhere in the cache. Therefore, the MySQL server can directly send the response without processing the request.

Using a memory-based filesystem for caching (Become an expert)

We can easily say that the slowest component of a computer is its hard drive. Moreover, the Magento caching system makes massive use of this component. It would be amazing if we could store the Magento cache files directly inside the memory.

How to do it...

Open a new console on your Unix server and enter the following command:

```
sudo mount -t tmpfs -o size=256M,mode=0777 tmpfs /var/www/YOUR_DOMAIN.COM/var/cache/
```

> The path is based on a common installation of Apache with Magento; pay attention to your configuration when typing this command.

You have to repeat this command every time the server starts up or you can automatize it by adding the following line into your /etc/fstab file:

```
tmpfs /var/www/YOUR_DOMAIN.COM/var/cache/ tmpfs size=256,mode=0777 0 0
```

All the caching mechanisms of Magento will now work with a memory-based filesystem instead of the classical filesystem.

How it works...

This newly created filesystem is intended to appear as a mounted filesystem, but takes place in the RAM. Of course, the access time of this kind of filesystem is extremely slow in comparison with a classical hard drive. However, all files updated or created are temporary because of the nature of this filesystem. Nothing will be written in the hard drive, and if you reboot everything will be lost. If you plan to reboot your server, you have to save the volatile files in your hard drive, unmount the memory-based system, and then copy the saved data from `tmpfs` in the cache folder. With the second command, the folder will be remounted automatically after the reboot.

Compressing your code – gzip (Become an expert)

In this recipe, we will use algorithms that are able to compress and uncompress textual data, such as the HTML code behind our web pages.

Getting ready

If you host your Magento website on a dedicated server and you have all of the rights on your web server, just locate your `php.ini` and make sure you have the following line:

```
Zlib.output_compression on
```

If your host is shared it will be a bit of a challenge, but it's still possible!

How to do it...

In this recipe, we will compress our web pages by almost 80 percent. To do this, find the file named `.htaccess` in the root directory of your Magento installation and open it with your favorite text editor. Remove the sharp at line 52 so it looks like the following:

```
## enable resulting html compression

    php_flag zlib.output_compression on
```

When it's done, go to line 74 and find the block belonging to `mod_deflate.c`. Then remove the sharps at lines 81, 86, 89, 92, 95, and 98 so that it looks like the following:

```
<IfModule mod_deflate.c>

    # Insert filter on all content
    SetOutputFilter DEFLATE
    # Insert filter on selected content types only
```

```
#AddOutputFilterByType DEFLATE text/html text/plain text/xml
text/css text/javascript

# Netscape 4.x has some problems...
BrowserMatch ^Mozilla/4 gzip-only-text/html

# Netscape 4.06-4.08 have some more problems
BrowserMatch ^Mozilla/4\.0[678] no-gzip

# MSIE masquerades as Netscape, but it is fine
BrowserMatch \bMSIE !no-gzip !gzip-only-text/html

# Don't compress images
SetEnvIfNoCase Request_URI \.(?:gif|jpe?g|png)$ no-gzip dont-
vary

# Make sure proxies don't deliver the wrong content
Header append Vary User-Agent env=!dont-vary
```

```
</IfModule>
```

Find the file named `php.ini.sample` in the root directory of Magento and rename it to `php.ini`; then remove the comma at line 19.

```
; enable resulting html compression

zlib.output_compression = on
```

The previous size of our HTML file was 25.16 KB and it has folded to 4.37 KB with these manipulations. You can check what the compression offers you by visiting this website: `http://www.gidnetwork.com/tools/gzip-test.php`. However, the total weight of our home page was 713.4 KB; so the compression of HTML files is not so significant in comparison with the total weight.

The total weight is divided into four parts. There is the JavaScript of 360 KB, the CSS of 100 KB, the HTML of 25.16 KB before compression, and images of 218.2 KB. From the perspective of a computer, HTML, JavaScript, and CSS are very similar: they are just bunches of text. So, with a few more steps we will be able to compress our JavaScript and our CSS in the same way as HTML.

With JavaScript and CSS compression still enabled, perform the following steps:

1. Create a file named `info.php` that contains `<?php phpinfo(); ?|`

   Upload this new file (`info.php`) to your web server and browse to the file. When the page is fully loaded, search for DOCUMENT_ROOT. This value is the exact path of your server, and it can be tricky to find the path on a shared hosting environment.

2. Create a file named `php.ini` that contains the following lines of code:

    ```
    zlib.output_compression=1
    auto_prepend_file=VALUE_FROM_STEP_ONE/media/gzip.php
    ```

    Upload the newly created file, `php.ini`, in `MAGENTO_HOME/media/css/` and in `MAGENTO_HOME/media/js/`.

3. Create a file named `gzip.php` that contains the following lines of code:

    ```php
    <?php
    if (isset($_SERVER['SCRIPT_FILENAME'])) {
        echo "/*".$_SERVER['SCRIPT_FILENAME']."*/";
        $timestamp = filemtime(__FILE__);
        header('Last-Modified: ' . $timestamp);
        $expires = 60*60*24*14;
        header("Pragma: public");
        header("Cache-Control: maxage=".$expires);
        header('Expires:'.gmdate('D,d M Y
            H:i:s',time()+$expires).'GMT');
        header('Vary: Accept-Encoding');
        $pathinfo = pathinfo($_SERVER['SCRIPT_FILENAME']);
        $extension = $pathinfo['extension'];
        if ($extension == 'css') {
            header('Content-type: text/css');
        }
        if ($extension == 'js') {
            header('Content-type: text/javascript');
        }
    }?
    ```

4. Check if it works!

Browse back to `http://www.gidnetwork.com/tools/gzip-test.php` and test the direct address of your CSS files and JavaScript files. In theory, your files should be compressed and a new line with the filename should appear as the first line of your CSS and JavaScript files. If they are not compressed, reopen your `.htaccess` file in the root directory of Magento and add the following line of code at the top:

```
AddType x-mapp-php5 .php .shtml .html .htm .txt .js .css
```

This line can totally mess up your CSS; therefore, we add the following line just after the previous line:

```
RemoveHandler .css
```

It's done! Let's have a look at the performance after compressing all of your content:

Type	Requests	Load time	Size (KB)
CSS	1	35 milliseconds	110.6
CSS compressed	1	30 milliseconds	21
JS	1	62 milliseconds	360
JS compressed	1	50 milliseconds	85.8
Overall	35	1.12 seconds	713.4
Overall compressed	35	993 milliseconds	330.3

As before, the total weight is divided into four parts but the percentages have changed. Now JavaScript stands for 85.8 KB, the CSS for 21 KB, the HTML for 4.37 KB, and the images for 218.2 KB. We've just found a way to compress our web pages by 54 percent, and as a result optimize the overall load time.

How it works...

gzip is a GNU project used (initiated in 1992) for compression and decompression. It's based on the DEFLATE algorithm and enables compressing textual data, such as HTML, CSS, and JavaScript by 80 percent. A common misconception is that compressing textual data when the customer requests it will slow down the server. Indeed, it does take CPU time to do the compression, but the result is that your server runs with notably less data and reduces the CPU load.

Installing a PHP accelerator (Become an expert)

In this recipe we will learn how to improve performance of any application written in PHP by creating a brand new caching system. This recipe is relevant only if your server stands on a dedicated server and you have a root access to it.

How to do it...

1. We will install **Alternative PHP Cache** (**APC**) on our Unix-based server. In order to install this caching system on our server, we will need to import several packages, as done in the following command line:

   ```
   sudo apt-get install php-pear php5-dev apache2-threaded-dev make
   ```

2. When all these packages are successfully installed, we can go ahead and install APC by using the following command:

   ```
   sudo pecl install apc-3.1.4
   ```

3. Then you have to create a file named `apc.ini` under `/etc/php5/conf.d/`. Add the following content in the newly created file:

```
extension=apc.so
```

4. Create a file named `info.php` that contains the following code and upload it:

```
<?php phpinfo(); ?|
```

5. Open `local.xml` under `/app/etc/` and locate the following line:

```
<global>
```

6. Then add the following lines after the previous line:

```
<cache>
    <backend>apc</backend>
    <prefix>yourStoreName</prefix>
</cache>
```

7. Restart your web server.

The Alternative PHP cache should now be installed on your server; you can check if it's working correctly by browsing to the `info.php` file. If there is an APC section, it means that everything is done correctly.

Using the same web stressor, the Apache benchmarking tool, we will compare the performance when our PHP accelerator is on and when it is off.

Type	Min (milliseconds)	Max (milliseconds)	Median (milliseconds)	Requests/second
APC off	432	744	452	2.17
APC on	231	686	268	3.54

Another relevant improvement! Indeed, median time to complete a request was reduced by almost 40 percent. So your server can now handle 3.54 requests per second, which is almost a 60 percent improvement!

How it works...

PHP accelerators are extensions made for improving the performance of any application written with PHP. The main aim is to cache the PHP byte code in order to skip all the parsing and compiling processes when a processor executes PHP scripts. The cached code uses the shared memory so that it can be executed from there. On an average, the improvements that come with a PHP accelerator vary by two or seven.

Clustering (Become an expert)

If you have successfully applied all the techniques already presented and your Magento is still slow, it means that you are a very prosperous online retailer and it's time to leave the comfortable world where there is a single server. To keep your customers satisfied, you have to invest in hardware; the tweaking time is now over.

Getting ready

Let's begin with a little bit of general knowledge on clustering. If you are used to it, you can definitively skip to the next *How to do it...* section. In all recipes related to clustering we will use four images to illustrate architectures. They represent a user, web server, CDN, and a database server.

Most Magento owners will fit into two categories. The ones in the first will have a dedicated server that contains all the Magento needs.

In this configuration, a browser will accede to your server through the Internet and the DNS mechanism, which is beyond the scope of this recipe. This single server contains:

- A web server with Magento
- A database server
- Images, CSS, and scripts

The ones in the second category of Magento owners have a separate database server. Typically, people who have a shared hosting environment have their databases hosted on another server (which is also shared). In this configuration, all resources belonging to servers are dedicated to a specific task.

How to do it...

If you own a single server, you can begin by separating your database in a dedicated server. In order to do this, you have to invest in another server and install MySQL on it (get your host to do it for you), and then extract your database from your first server and import it to your new server. Magento stays on your first server; you have to modify the database connection. Go to `/app/etc/local.xml` and modify the following lines to fit the new server parameters:

```
<connection>|
    <host>|<![CDATA[NEW_SERVER_ADDRESS]]>|</host>|
    <username>|<![CDATA[NEW_USER_NAME]]>|</username>|
    <password>|<![CDATA[NEW_PASSWORD]]>|</password>|
    <dbname>|<![CDATA[NEW DATABASE_NAME]]>|</dbname>|
    <initStatements>|<![CDATA[SET NAMES utf8]]>|</initStatements>|
    <model>|<![CDATA[mysql4]]>|</model>|
    <type>|<![CDATA[pdo_mysql]]>|</type>|
    <pdoType>|<![CDATA[]]>|</pdoType>|
    <active>|1</active>|
</connection>|
```

As simple as that. You now use a dedicated database server and improve your store performance.

The second step in clustering our environment could be using a CDN for our images, CSS, and scripts. A CDN is an independent server optimized for delivering static content such as images, CSS, and scripts. In this way, our web server can focus on running Magento and the CDN can focus on displaying static content. The good news is that Magento has native support to do this.

In your Magento backend, navigate to **System | General | Web | Unsecure**.

Unsecure		⌃
Base URL	http://mathieu-nayrolles.com/magento-performanc	[STORE VIEW]
Base Link URL	{{unsecure_base_url}}	[STORE VIEW]
Base Skin URL	{{unsecure_base_url}}skin/	[STORE VIEW]
Base Media URL	MY_CDN_ADDRESS/media/	[STORE VIEW]

If you still have CSS and JavaScript compressed from the previous recipes, you just have to copy your media directory from your main server to your CDN server. If it's not the case anymore, you have to modify the **Base Skin URL** field and the **Base JavaScript URL** field. Also, if for some reason you use the secure URL for that kind of content, don't forget to apply the changes to the secure part as well.

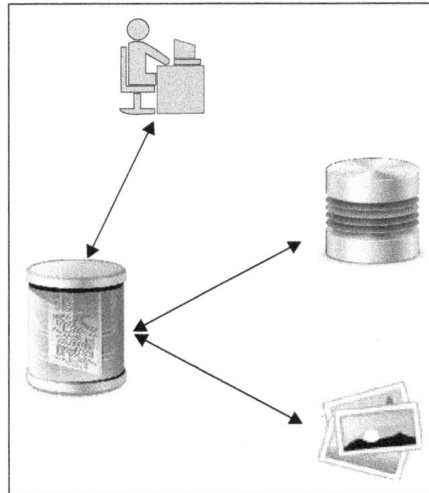

How it works...

That's a very good start. Let's summarize it. We were using a single server for all requests, and now, depending on the request, we use three different servers. The first one handles all the Magento work for building pages, the second one handles the data-related operations, and the last one provides static content. With this kind of architecture, each server can focus on only one purpose.

Balancing load (Become an expert)

What could be the next major improvement in clustering our environment? Get more and more web servers to take care of the heavy work due to the generation of pages.

How to do it...

Our aim in this recipe is to build an architecture where our customers accede to one unique server, but this server is able to balance requests on other servers depending on their current load.

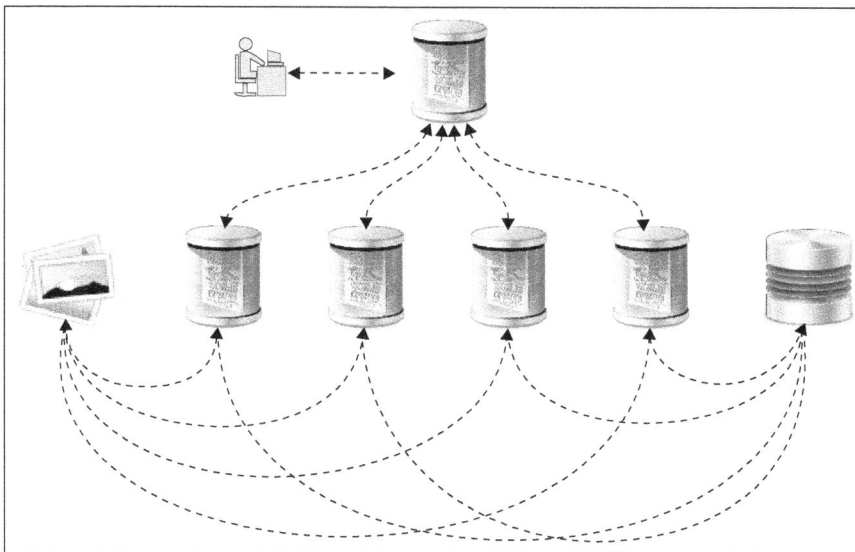

Each server belonging to the second layer of servers is an exact replica of your Magento server. You can either reinstall your web server and Magento on each one or ask your hosting company to deliver you an exact replica of the old one. The real work is on the front server, the one to which your customers accede. We have to install a piece of software called reverse proxy in order to forward requests from this frontend server to every backend server.

Open a new terminal and enter the following command:

```
sudo apt-get install pound
```

Then edit the file named `pound.cfg` in the `/etc/pound/` directory so that it looks like the following code:

```
ListenHTTP
  Address 10.0.0.1 #FRONT SERVER ADDRESS
  Port 80

  Service
    BackEnd
      Address 10.0.0.2 #MY FIRST BACKEND SERVER
      Port 80
```

```
      End
      BackEnd
        Address 10.0.0.3 # MY SECOND BACKEND SERVER
        Port 80
      End
      #REPEAT BACKEND BLOCKS FOR EACH SERVERS
    END
  END
```

Enable the frontend server to start by modifying the value of `Startup` in `/etc/default/pound` as follows:

```
Startup = 1
```

Then start the frontend server using the following command and it will switch from one server to another, depending on the load:

```
Sudo /etc/init.d/pound start
```

How it works...

The idea behind this well-known technique, named load balancing, is to get one server in front of the others and for that server to redirect users to the least loaded servers at that moment. Moreover, you have web servers behind this one; so each of them will be less loaded.

Replicating the database (Become an expert)

After getting a bunch of new web servers, we probably could increase the number of database servers; but how to ensure the data integrity if two or more servers want to write new data at the same time?

Getting ready

What we aim at in this recipe is database replication with a master database and slave database(s).

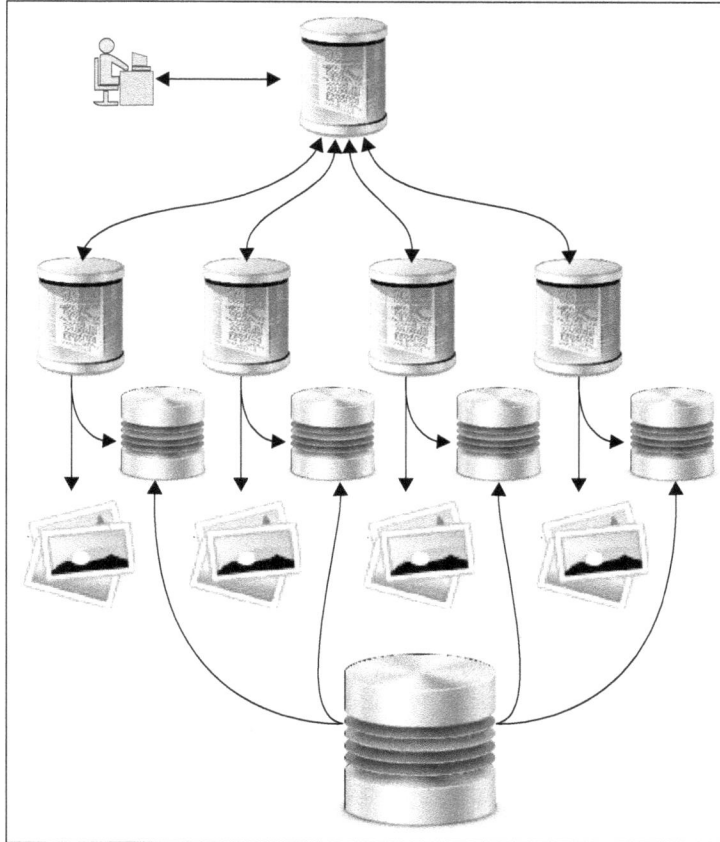

In this architecture, each database belonging to one web server is called a **slave database**, and they can only retrieve data. They will handle most of the data-related operations, because there is very little new data in Magento (such as new articles and orders). When a web server has to write something, it will do it in the master database (the big one; for the sake of readability, the communication arrows between web servers and the master database are not shown). The block that comprises one web server, one database server, and one CDN server is for reference only. Indeed, you have to adjust the number of servers to your traffic. You could need only one database server for three web servers and only one CDN server. Installations and configurations of MySQL databases and their replications are not treated here. You can find an excellent tutorial on database replication at `http://www.howtoforge.com/mysql_database_replication`.

How to do it...

In order to replicate the database, we have to configure our Magento servers on our different web servers with two database connections. The first one for writing—this one will be the same for all our servers—and a second one for reading. The reading connection could change if you have many other MySQL servers. Locate and modify the following bunch of code in `app/etc/local.xml`:

```
<default_setup>
<connection>
    <host><![CDATA[MASTER_SERVER_ADDRESS]]></host>
    <username><![CDATA[MASTER_USER_NAME]]></username>
    <password><![CDATA[MASTER_PASSWORD]]></password>
    <dbname><![CDATA[MASTER_DATABASE_NAME]]></dbname>
    <initStatements><![CDATA[SET NAMES utf8]]></initStatements>
    <model><![CDATA[mysql4]]></model>
    <type><![CDATA[pdo_mysql]]></type>
    <pdoType><![CDATA[]]></pdoType>
    <active>1</active>
</connection>
</default_setup>
```

Then add the highlighted lines that follow:

```
<default_read>
<connection>
    <host><![CDATA[SLAVE_SERVER_ADDRESS]]></host>
    <username><![CDATA[SLAVE_USER_NAME]]></username>
    <password><![CDATA[SLAVE_PASSWORD]]></password>
    <dbname><![CDATA[SLAVE_DATABASE_NAME]]></dbname>
    <initStatements><![CDATA[SET NAMES utf8]]></initStatements>
    <model><![CDATA[mysql4]]></model>
    <type><![CDATA[pdo_mysql]]></type>
    <pdoType><![CDATA[]]></pdoType>
    <active>1</active>
</connection>
</default_read>
```

All your Magento servers will now write to the master database and read information from the slave servers.

Let's have a look at our website if we turn on all the options we studied before:

- ▶ All the options in the previous recipes
- ▶ Turn on Expires
- ▶ Turn on KeepAlive

- Turn on the sessions in the database
- Turn on MySQL tuned on a dedicated server
- Turn on the memory-based filesystem for the cache directory
- Turn on gzip

Due to hardware limitations, we cannot benchmark the following settings:

- Load balancing
- Database replication

Type	Requests	Load time	Size (KB)
CSS (before)	1	35 milliseconds	110.6
CSS (after)	1	30 milliseconds	21
JS (before)	1	62 milliseconds	360
JS (after)	1	50 milliseconds	85.8
Overall (before)	35	1.12 seconds	713.4
Overall (after)	35	662 milliseconds	330.3

With this recipe, we have increased the loading time by 41 percent and reduced the size by 53 percent. Compared with our first launch in this book, we have won almost two full seconds in displaying exactly the same page.

All your servers are fully configured to focus on performance and your Magento is faster than light! Everything is now ready to keep your innumerable customers satisfied.

In the next recipes we will learn how to use several debugging tools with the aim of finding out where the problems are and being able to choose the appropriate solutions. The tools you'll learn to use are the same as the ones that we used to find more appropriate settings in the previous recipes.

In the past recipes, we have used several tools for identifying the best settings of our Magento instances. These tools have enabled us to find the most adapted tweaks, tips, and tricks in order to speed up our servers. In the coming recipes, you will learn what these amazing tools are and how to use them.

Checking the configuration (Must know)

The best way to give up on Magento is to let your configuration mislead you.

How to do it...

Check if your configuration scope is well parameterized.

Go to **System | Configuration**.

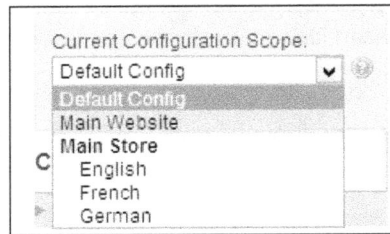

In the top-right corner, check if the current scope corresponds to the attending scope. If not, select the right one and save your configuration in the top-right corner.

How it works...

Because Magento offers the possibility to administrators to get as many configurations as a Magento store, we have to be careful about the current one.

Clearing caches (Must know)

Like we saw before, caching mechanisms store data for a faster retrieve. This data can be outdated and can mislead you in finding bugs.

How to do it...

The first step is to answer the question, "Why is this not working?". The answer to this is to clear all caches.

Go to **System | Cache Management**.

Cache Type	Description	Associated Tags	Status
☑ Configuration	System(config.xml, local.xml) and modules configuration files(config.xml).	CONFIG	ENABLED
☑ Layouts	Layout building instructions.	LAYOUT_GENERAL_CACHE_TAG	ENABLED
☑ Blocks HTML output	Page blocks HTML.	BLOCK_HTML	ENABLED
☑ Translations	Translation files.	TRANSLATE	ENABLED
☐ Collections Data	Collection data files.	COLLECTION_DATA	DISABLED
☐ EAV types and attributes	Entity types declaration cache.	EAV	DISABLED
☐ Web Services Configuration	Web Services definition files (api.xml).	CONFIG_API	DISABLED
☐ Web Services Configuration	Web Services definition files (api2.xml).	CONFIG_API2	DISABLED

Select all enabled caches and refresh them by selecting **Refresh** in the top-right corner and finally click on the **Submit** button. Lastly, clear your browser cache.

How it works...

The caching mechanism that we studied before stores responses rather than computing them. If you change something in your configuration, it's highly probable that your browser or the Magento caching system still stores the old responses. Indeed, retrieving outdated data from your caching systems can mislead you in finding bugs.

There's more...

Sometimes you will have to make sure that all the caches are actually clean. The only way to be sure is to delete them manually.

Deleting the cache from filesystem

There is another option for deleting the cache belonging to Magento. You have to delete the cache directory under YOUR_STORE.COM/var.

Logging (Must know)

Check what Magento tells us about the bug you are confronting.

How to do it...

Go to **System** | **Configuration** | **Advanced** | **Developer** | **Log Settings**.

Log Settings			
Enabled	Yes	⌄	[STORE VIEW]

Select **Yes** from the drop-down menu and save your configuration in the top-right corner. From this moment, all actions done by Magento will be stored in two files, system.log and exception.log, under YOUR_STORE.COM/var/log.

How it works...

Every time the instruction Mage::log ("your log") is called, a line is written in system.log, and in exception.log when Mage::logException ("your exception") is called. You can use the native one for debugging your Magento or place a customized one where you need it.

There's more...

Here, you will find some tips about how to allow your web server to write a log and how to locate the web server logs.

Permission for the web server

Don't forget to apply `chmod 0777` on the `var/logs` directory to allow your web server to write data there.

Apache error_log

When you can't find the answer you're looking for in the Magento log, have a look at Apache's `error_log`. Indeed, your errors could belong to your web server.

Using template hints (Must know)

In this recipe we will learn how to display template-related information for debugging purposes.

How to do it...

Go to **System | Configuration | Advanced | Developer | Debug**.

Debug			⌃
Profiler	No	⌄	[STORE VIEW]
Template Path Hints	Yes	⌄	[STORE VIEW]
Add Block Names to Hints	Yes	⌄	[STORE VIEW]

Turn on both the **Template Path Hints** and **Add Block Names to Hints** fields, and then save your configuration in the top-right corner.

If these options are not available at your backend, open and modify the `system.xml` file under the `YOUR_STORE.COM/app/code/core/Mage/Core/etc/` directory at line 512 so that it looks like the following:

```
<template_hints translate="label">
  <label>Template Path Hints</label>
  <frontend_type>select</frontend_type>
  <source_model>adminhtml/system_config_source_yesno
  </source_model>
  <sort_order>20</sort_order>
  <show_in_default>1</show_in_default>
  <show_in_website>1</show_in_website>
```

```
    <show_in_store>1</show_in_store>
  </template_hints>

  <template_hints_blocks translate="label">
    <label>Add Block Names to Hints</label>
    <frontend_type>select</frontend_type>
    <source_model>adminhtml/system_config_source_yesno
    </source_model>
    <sort_order>21</sort_order>
    <show_in_default>1</show_in_default>
    <show_in_website>1</show_in_website>
    <show_in_store>1</show_in_store>
  </template_hints_blocks>
```

The lines to be modified are the ones that are highlighted. Then you can come back to your administration site and activate these options.

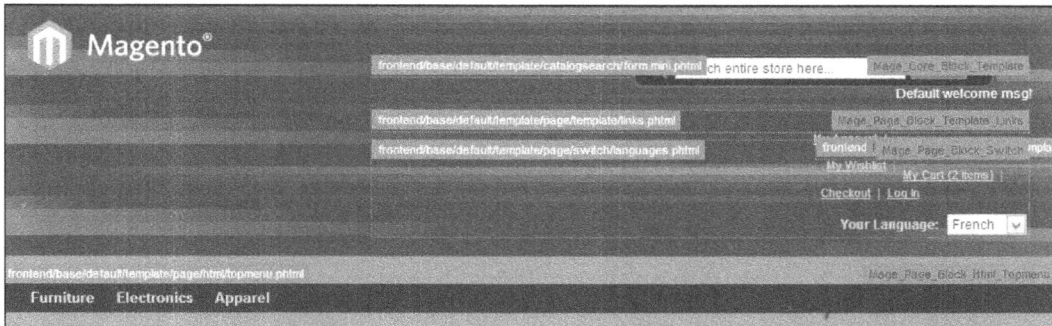

As you can see in the previous image, each part of our Magento now contains the name and the path of the responsible HTML or PHTML file. With this information, it will be easier to identify where the problems are.

How it works...

The Magento Core adds an HTML `<div>` tag before each file in order to build the final page with a specific case. This new HTML `<div>` tag contains the filename and the file path in order to locate it easily. Then, when you browse to it, the previous `<div>` tag is displayed.

Using the Profiler (Should know)

Magento embeds a library to profile your Magento and detect some performance issues. In this recipe, we will see how to use it.

How to do it...

1. Activate the Profiler by navigating to **System | Configuration | Advanced | Developer | Debug**.

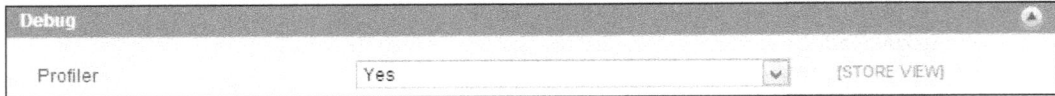

Debug			⌃
Profiler	Yes	⌄	[STORE VIEW]

2. The second step is to enable the debugger in YOUR_STORE.COM/index.php near line 71 and remove the sharp so that it looks like the following:

```
Varien_Profiler::enable();
```

If you can't find this line anywhere, add it somewhere before the last line (Mage::run($mageRunCode, $mageRunType);). If you have successfully enabled the profile, all your web pages will have a new footer similar to the following:

Memory usage: real: 26738688, emalloc: 26547220

Code Profiler	Time	Cnt	Emalloc	RealMem
mage	0.6248	1	0	0
CORE::create_object_of::Mage_Core_Model_Cache	0.0026	1	191,396	262,144
mage::app::init::config::load_cache	0.0059	1	2,444	0
mage::app::init::stores	0.0417	1	270,820	262,144
CORE::create_object_of::Mage_Core_Model_Resource_Website_Collection	0.0289	1	114,148	0
DISPATCH EVENT:resource_get_tablename	0.0011	87	12,000	0
DISPATCH EVENT:core_collection_abstract_load_before	0.0002	12	1,780	0
DISPATCH EVENT:core_collection_abstract_load_after	0.0002	12	1,780	0

How it works...

The table in your footer contains five columns; the first one, Code Profiler, contains your timer name associated to the second column, Time, which is the time when this timer has been reached. The third column, Cnt, counts the number of times you launch the same timer. Finally, the last two columns, Emalloc and RealMem stand for the amount of memory allocated to PHP. The difference between those two is that the parameter true is passed to the second one and is not passed to the first one.

The most important column to look at is the Cnt column, because it counts the number of instances of a specific object. And to instantiate an object is time consuming. A high number in the Cnt columns could mean that you made customizations that led to unnecessary object instantiations.

There's more...

Using the built-in timers can be enough, but for an effective debug you should use your own.

Adding your own timer

In addition to the native information provided by the Profiler, you can add your own timer. In order to do this, open the file you want to monitor and add the following statements:

```
Varien_Profiler::start('my_timer');
[some suspicious php code]
Varien_Profiler::stop('my_timer');
```

Using a debugger (Should know)

In this recipe, we will install and learn how to use Xdebug for debugging our development system.

Getting ready

If you are on a Unix system, type the following command to install Xdebug:

```
sudo pecl install xdebug
```

If you are on a Windows system, you can download a compiled DLL from http://www.xdebug.org/ and place it under the `ext` directory of your PHP installation.

Then you have to add the mapping in your `php.ini` file.

For Unix, add the following mapping:

```
zend_extension= xdebug.so
```

And for Windows, add the following mapping:

```
zend_extension_ts="Absolute_path_of_my_php\ext\
my_just_downloaded_dll"
```

After restarting your web server, you can create a file named `phpinfo.php` that contains the following:

```
<?php phpinfo(); ?|
```

Magento 1.4 Themes Design

ISBN: 978-1-849514-80-4   Paperback: 292 pages

Customize the appearance of your Magento 1.4
e-commerce store with Magento's powerful theming
engine.

1. Install and configure Magento 1.4 and learn the
   fundamental principles behind Magento themes

2. Customize the appearance of your Magento
   1.4 e-commerce store with Magento's powerful
   theming engine by changing Magento templates,
   skin files and layout files

3. Change the basics of your Magento theme from
   the logo of your store to the color scheme of
   your theme

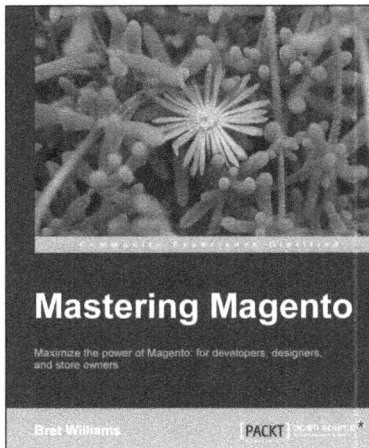

Mastering Magento

ISBN: 978-1-849516-94-5   Paperback: 300 pages

Maximize the power of Magento: for developers,
designers, and store owners

1. Learn how to customize your Magento store for
   maximum performance

2. Exploit little known techniques for extending and
   tuning your Magento installation.

3. Step-by-step guides for making your store run
   faster, better and more productively.

Please check **www.PacktPub.com** for information on our titles

Magento Mobile How-to

ISBN: 978-1-849693-66-0   Paperback: 78 pages

Create and configure your own Magento Mobile application and publish it for the Android and iOS platforms

1. Learn something new in an Instant! A short, fast, focused guide delivering immediate results.

2. Style and theme your Magento Mobile Application interface

3. Configure Product categories and add static content for mobile

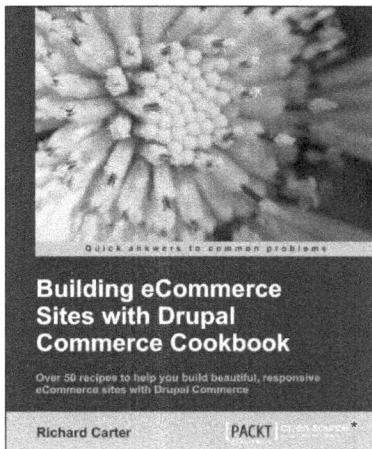

Building eCommerce Sites with Drupal Commerce Cookbook

ISBN: 978-1-782161-22-6   Paperback: 266 pages

Over 50 recipes to help you build beautiful, responsive eCommerce sites with Drupal Commerce

1. Learn how to build attractive eCommerce sites with Drupal Commerce

2. Customise your Drupal Commerce store for maximum impact

3. Reviewed by the creators of Drupal Commerce: The CommerceGuys

Please check **www.PacktPub.com** for information on our titles

www.ingramcontent.com/pod-product-compliance
Lightning Source LLC
Chambersburg PA
CBHW082113210326
41599CB00033B/6691